How The White Cube Hangs Once The Gallery Has Closed

Adam Blue

Stone House Press
247 Burr Road
Cornish, NH 03745

First Printing, 2012
Second Printing, 2014

ISBN: 1480083380
ISBN-13: 978-1480083387

This book is lovingly dedicated
to my family.

From my experience working in and around the arts, there are few genres that can make someone feel like they're in the wrong room faster than Minimalism.

Spend a day watching people walk through a museum where the galleries are hung by genre, and you'll observe different reactions in each of the different spaces. Some viewers might pause for sculptures made centuries ago in far away lands, and those who do may comment on the fables that the sculptures reference. In a gallery featuring impressionist paintings, you're likely to witness visitors talking about the saturated colors and gestural brush strokes in a piece. Whether or not a viewer likes classical sculpture or impressionist painting, they understand how to read them, and their relationship to art remains open and accessible. Then, observe an audience walk into a sterile-feeling, brightly lit chamber hosting a lone geometric shape, and you can watch people's eyebrows furrow. Before they leave, you can guess what they're thinking: Why should a white box, a neon bulb, or a checkerboard get a whole room in the museum? What makes this a masterpiece equal to the works I just saw in the other galleries?

Presenting Minimalist work as one genre among many can do more than bore an art audience: it can alienate them from visual art all together. Because logically, the next thoughts a person might have could be: if it's important enough to be in the museum and *I don't get what I see*, does everyone know something that I don't? Does that make me dumb? And if being here makes me feel stupid, then why am I here at all—this obviously isn't for me. Unfortunately, this unintended viewing experience is probably more common than anyone in the arts would like to admit.

The single most over-referenced quote about Minimalism is likely Frank Stella's "*What you see is what you see.*" Its popularity is justified, as I'll describe shortly. But, when this sentiment resonates wrongly, because what a person sees feels quotidian, overexposed, and distancing, that creates a problem for everyone. Because ultimately, when a museum visitor looks at a Minimalist piece, they see more than a questionable selection of institutionally empowered objects from a hardware store. They see a security guard observing them from the corner. And small groups of other people nodding sagely, with their arms crossed and a lone finger on their chin. And then they see the door.

The irony, of course, is that the founding Minimalist artists' intent was definitely related to, but very different from, this real-world reaction. Reading Donald Judd's *Specific Objects* (1964) and Robert Morris' *Notes on Sculpture* (1966) provides some primary document clues about the how and why of this work. Though Judd and Morris started from different places and arrived at similar outcomes, both had the ambition to try and bring the viewer's awareness more fully into the present moment, in both space and time. The artists hoped that by eliminating story-telling references from their work, viewers would not be conceptually transported into an imaginary world, effectively splitting them from their experience of that object in that space in that moment. The artists hoped that using industrially sourced materials would discourage the viewer from thinking about the expressive qualities implicitly found in handcrafted pieces. From their perspective, they could eliminate yet another distraction from the then and the there of that moment in time and space if the materials in their work were unaltered.

Paradoxically, in restricting the content and the form of their work for the ideational purity of a viewer's experience of space and time, the artists increased the importance of the work's context: the "neutral," white, privileged space that a formal art institution can uniquely provide. And though the authority of these institutional attributes was presumed to be an absolute truth sixty years ago, these assumptions sound pretty suspect when considered today...

Equally notable, as the content and form diminished in Minimalist art objects, the relative importance of what the artists, and others, wrote about their work exponentially increased. For a genre that sought the elegance of limited ornamentation, Minimalism had to wrap itself in an awful lot of words to cross the finish line. And, when you do read Judd and Morris' texts, another interesting wrinkle is revealed. For when they detail the philosophical roots of their creative inquiry, the artists cite trying to challenge the conventions found in the *paintings* of their day. So even though some of their most successful works were sculptures, the artists weren't overly concerned with engaging the tensions found within that discipline at that time.

▫ ☐ ▫

For *How The White Cube Hangs Once The Gallery Has Closed*, I thought I would play with some of Minimalism's core ideas as I've just described them.

With respect to the form this project took, I honored the Minimalist ambitions of using only raw, industrial materials. I salvaged six old window screens—each was roughly 34" on a side and their weathered white surfaces were achieved without my interference. I used thirty-two 1½" wood screws and sixteen 3" 90-degree mounting brackets to fashion the top and bottom faces, which when placed gently, could temporarily balance the screens in cube form.

I decided to invert the artists' ambition of removing all narrative content from the piece, feeling it would be more fun to ground the cube in everyday life than to imprison it in the over-valued sanctity of art spaces. So, I threw the stack of screens and a point-and-shoot camera in the trunk of my car, and spent a year driving the white cube around with me anywhere and everywhere I went, ready to be installed at any and all times, riffing literally on the all-times-and-all-spaces experience the Minimalists embraced. Figuring this process would allow me to populate its world with some of the humorous and critical moments I encountered, I also hoped it would create a way for viewers to sympathize with the modernist icon—a form that tried to remind us to live in the present, even if that meant pushing away life's meaningful gestures to bring our attention back to them.

Much to my amusement, a few months into this endeavor I realized that what started as a conceptual piece had turned into a photography project. And since it was a photography project, well, it ought to be about the boundaries defining contemporary sculpture. Where does it begin, and where does it end? What materials can be included, and what materials cannot? Who is it for, and what purpose might it serve? Who decides if it's good, and why?

And finally, as the Minimalists did before me, I've now formally buried this body of work in far too many words. Ha!

So without further ado, let's get to it. I hope you enjoy *How The White Cube Hangs Once The Gallery Has Closed*.

Perfectly camouflaged in space and time.
And workin' it 'til 5pm.

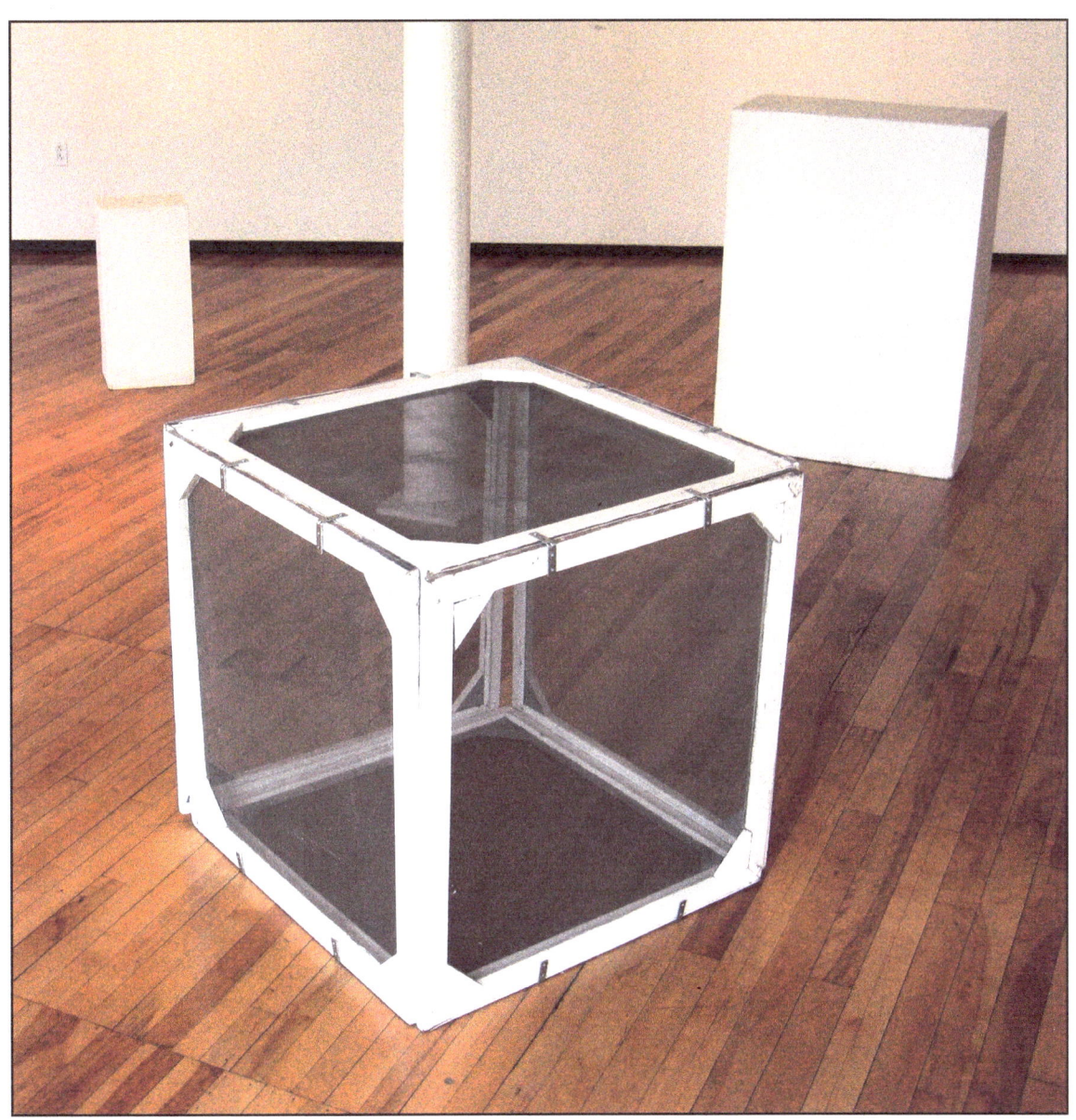

People think my older brother is awesome.
But he's cool.
I mean, we can still hang out and everything.

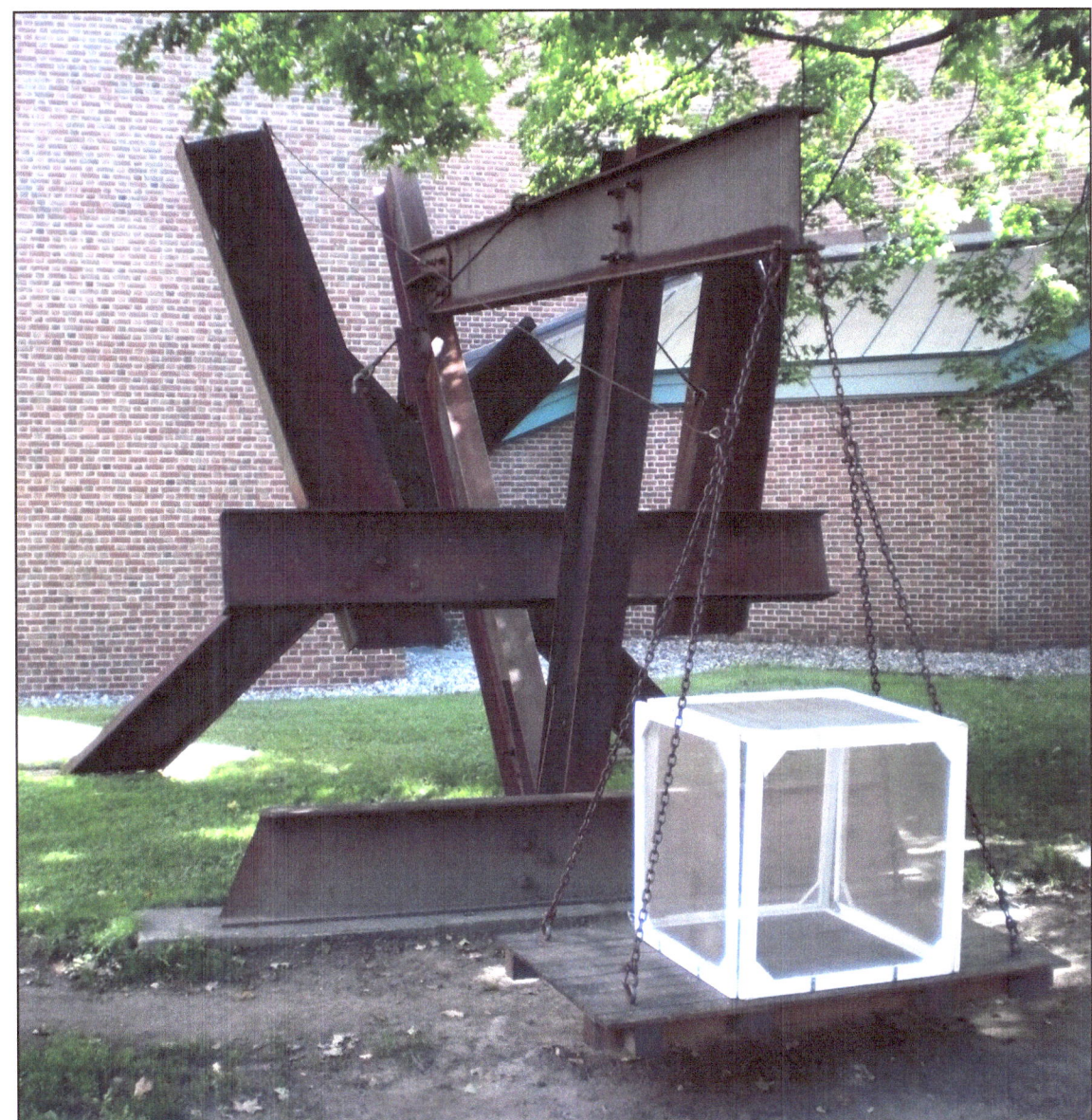

My mother says my uncle did
way too many drugs in the sixties.
But I don't know, he's great with kids.

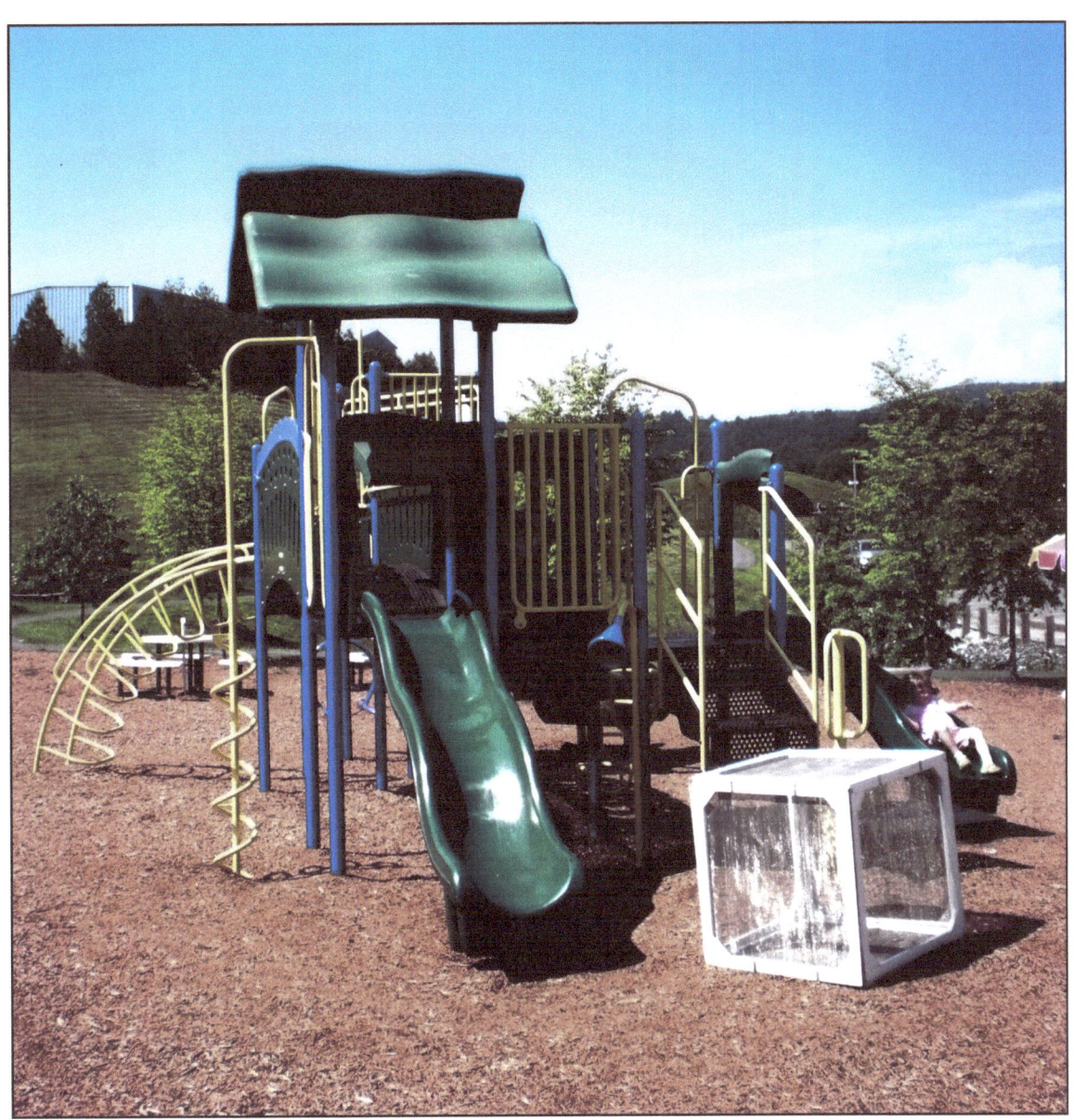

I love partying with these dudes.
They make me laugh and laugh and laugh.

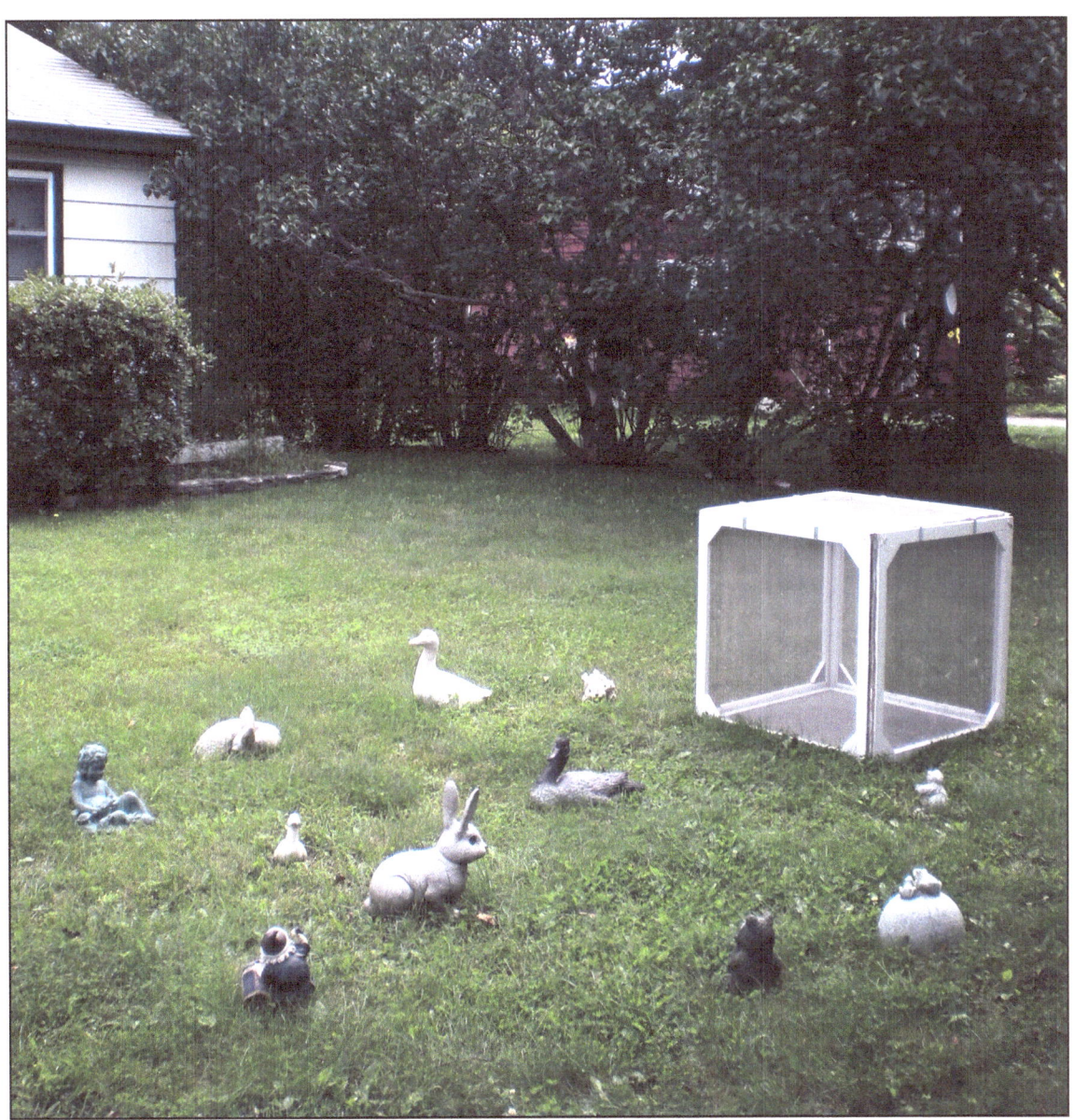

By making golf so expensive, they've really taken it away from the people.

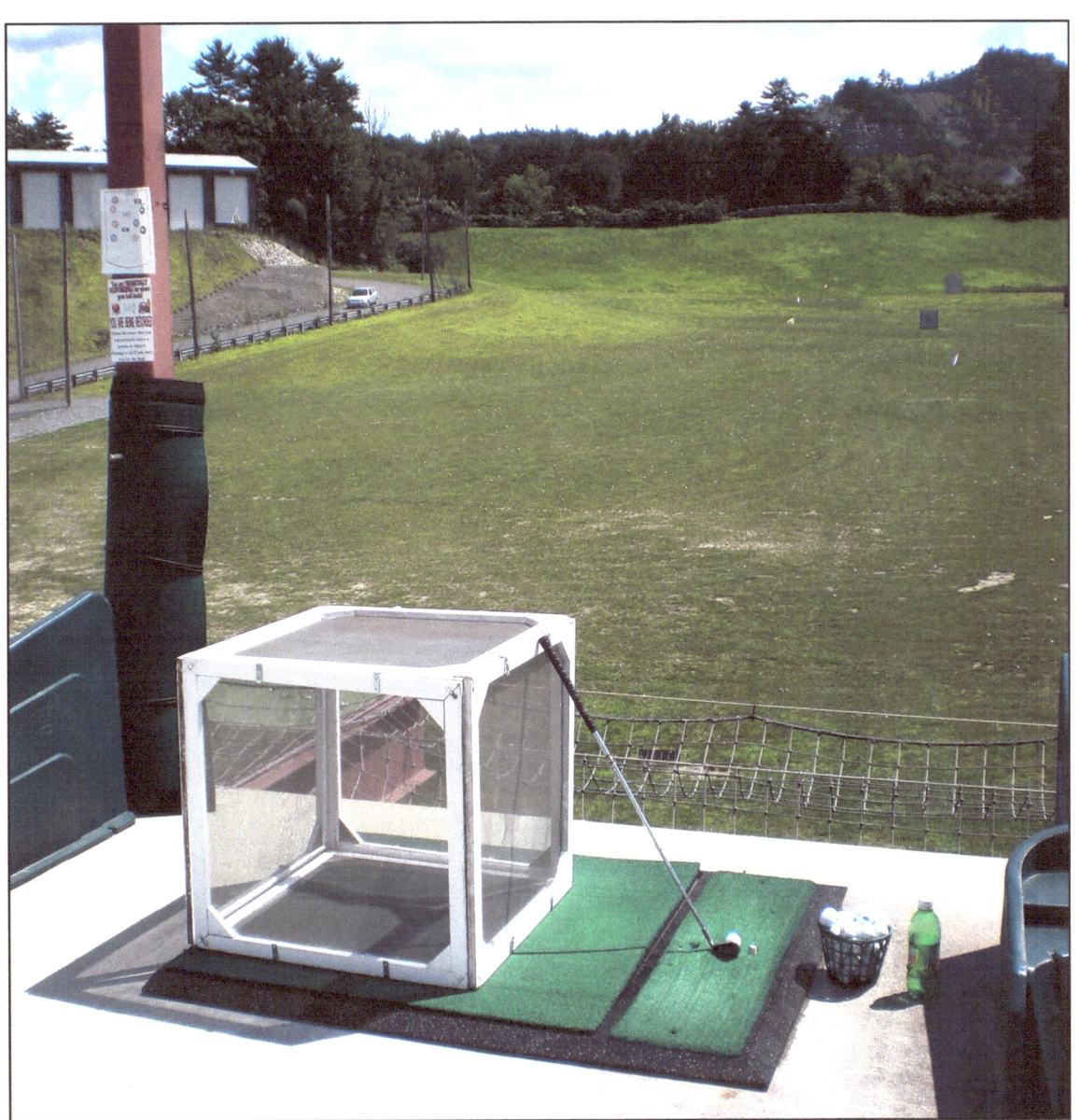

It's kinda weird being the oldest at the skate park.
But I'm good with it.

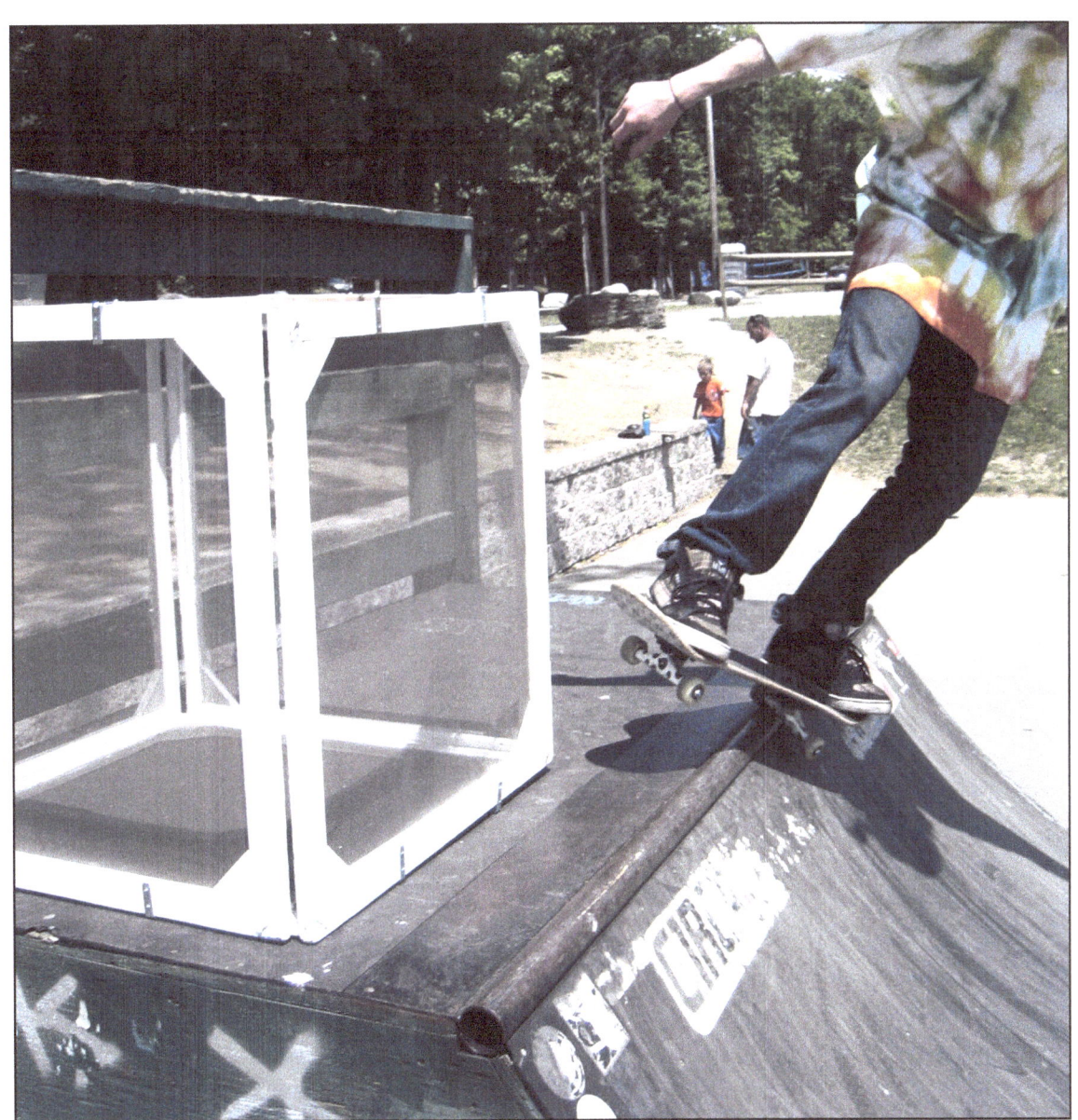

I'm the king of the mountain!
Oh wait, I'm alone.

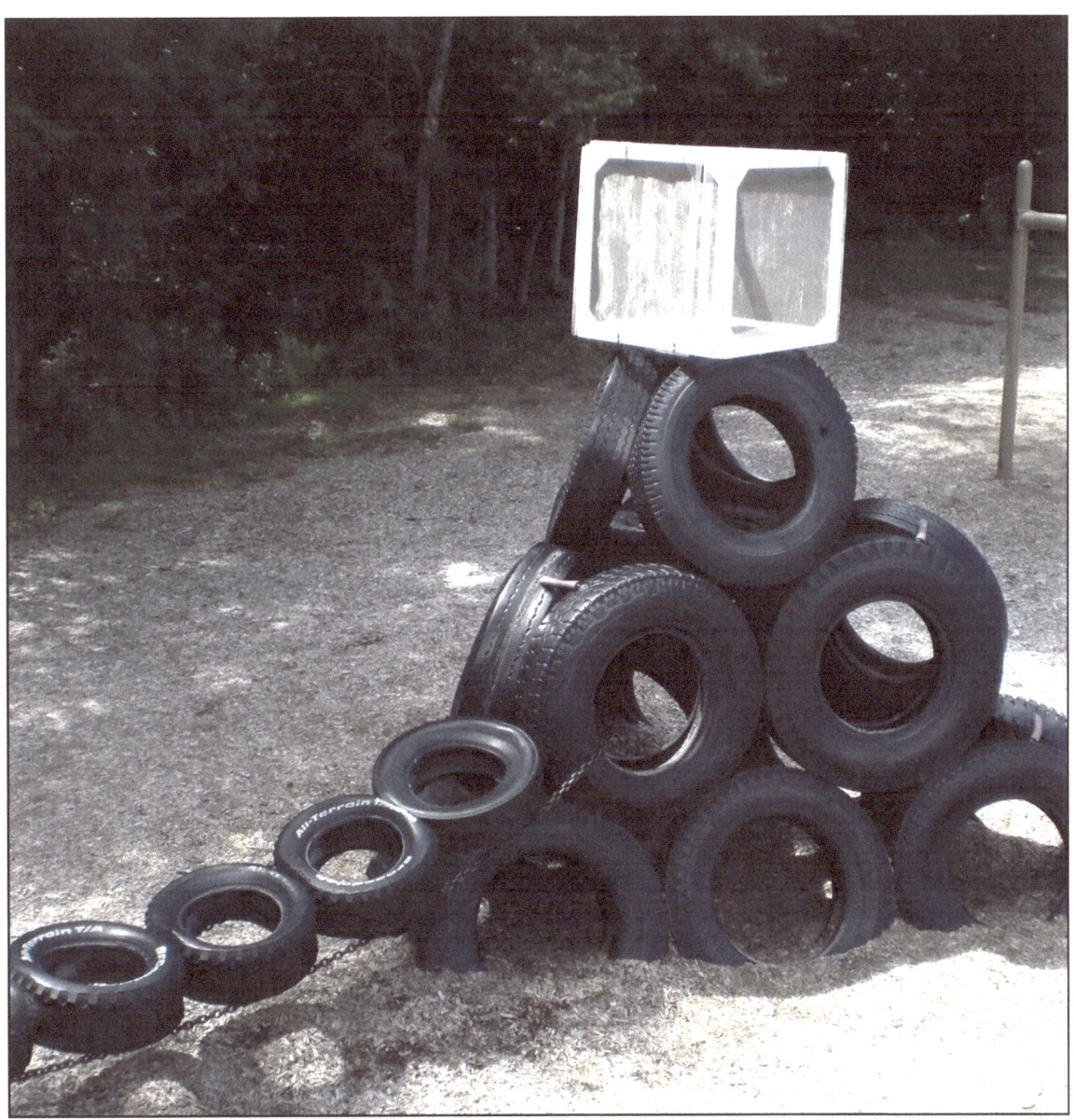

It's important to eat organic when you can.

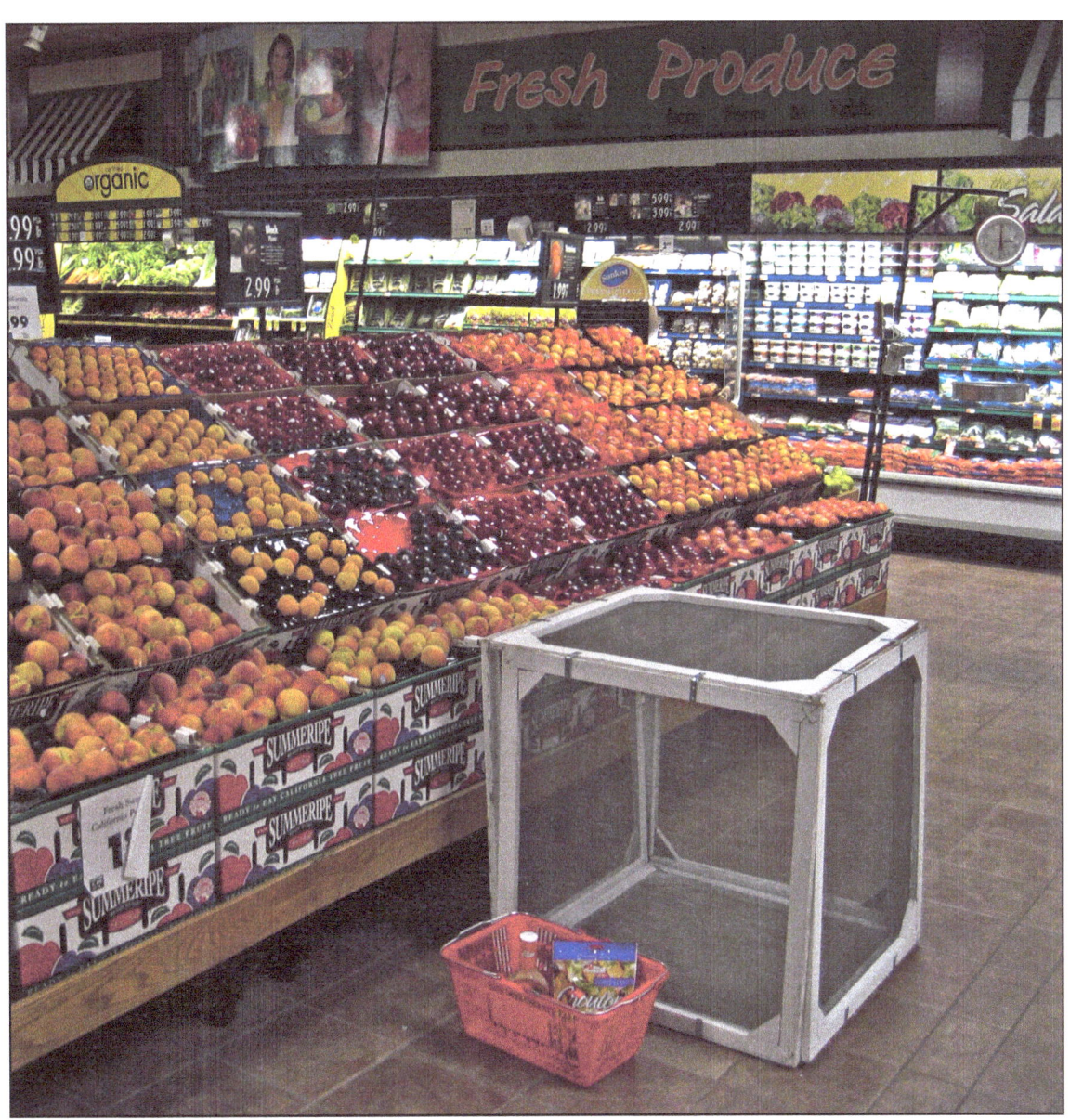

Ok, then. Just give me two baconators.

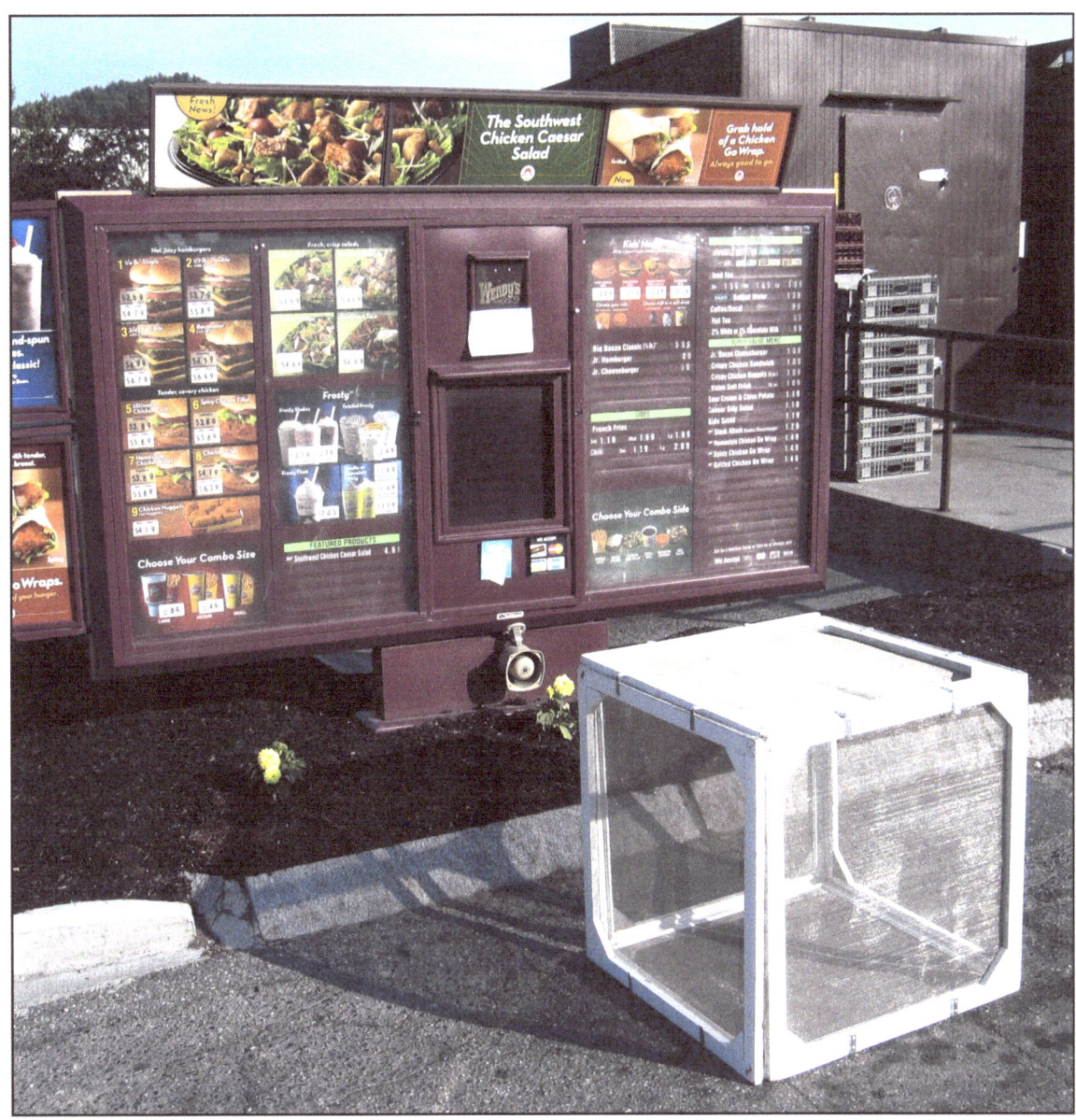

Time on the water really helps with my poetry.

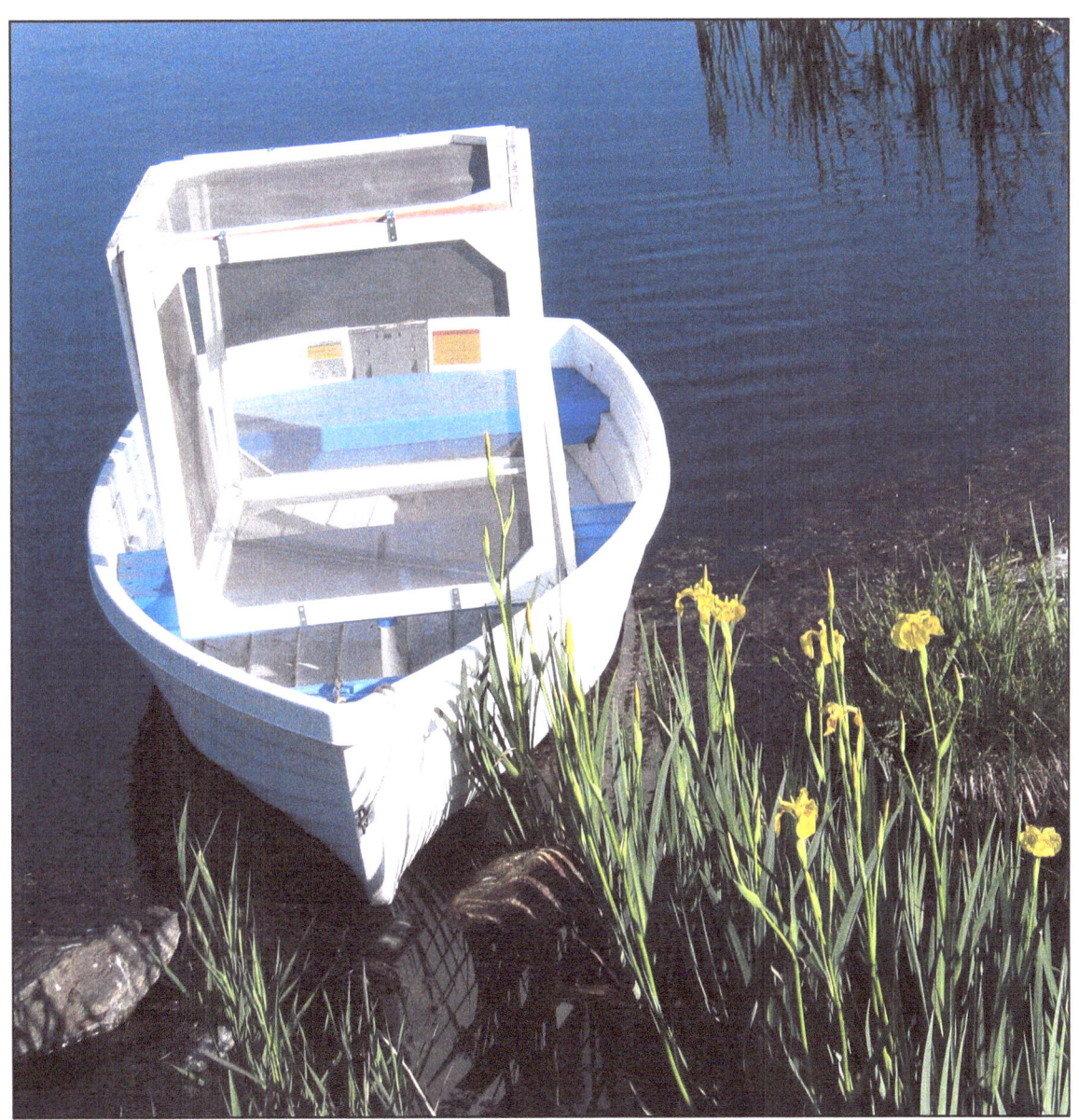

You have got to be fucking kidding me.

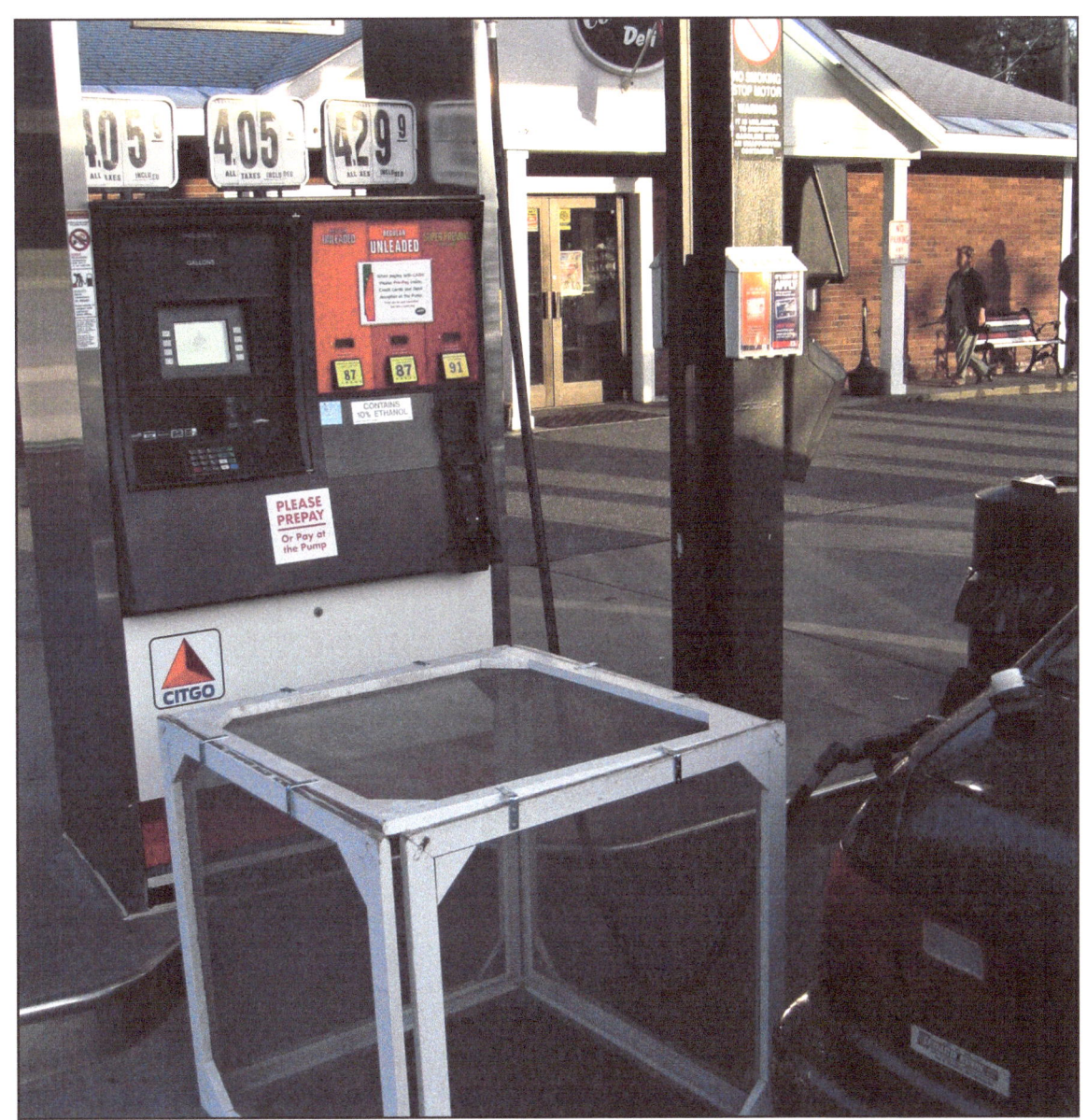

So, if a fulltime employee earns little enough
to qualify for food stamps...
Doesn't that mean our taxpayer dollars are
subsidizing their corporate profits?

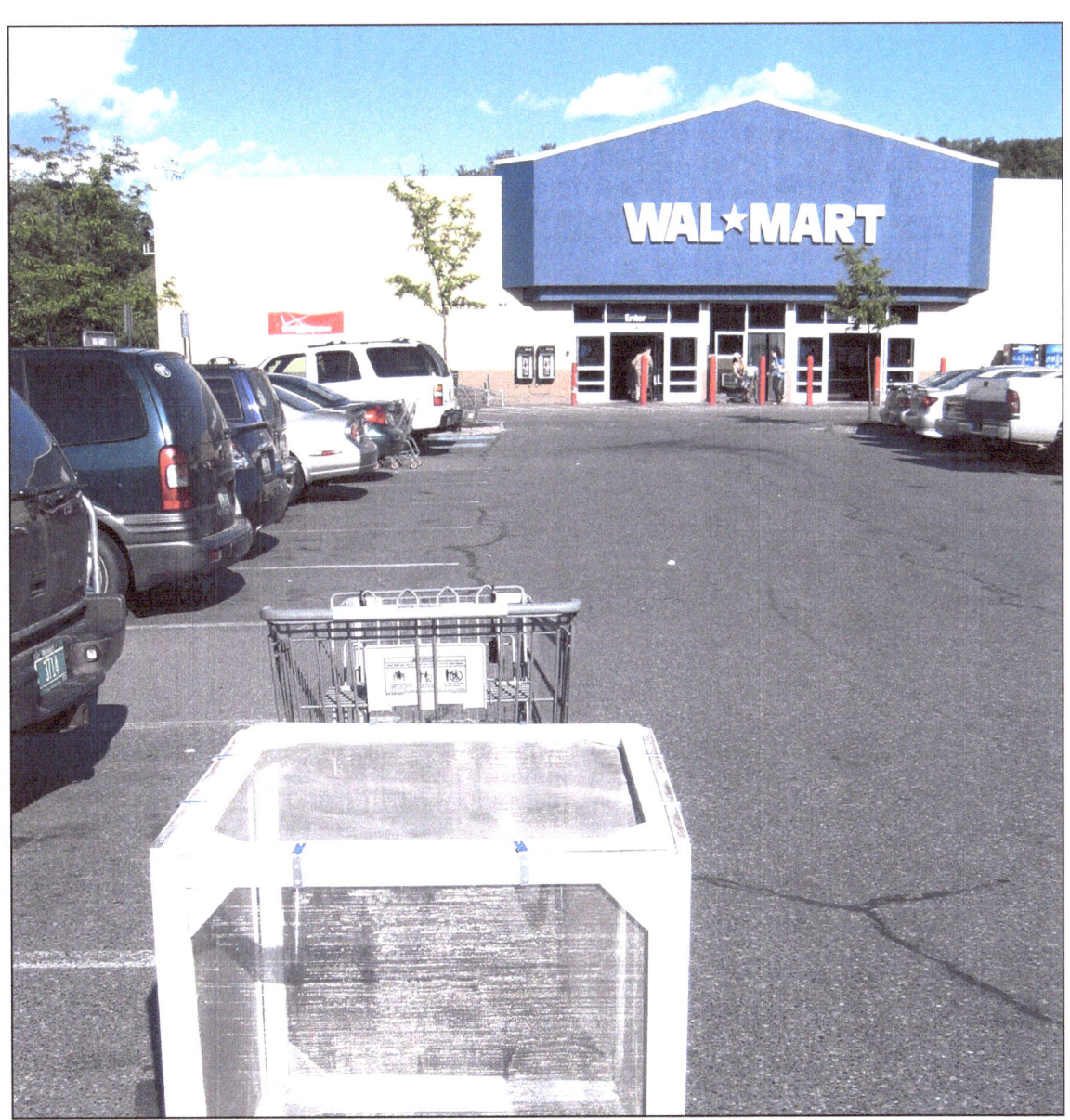

Raking leaves can be like, totally zen.

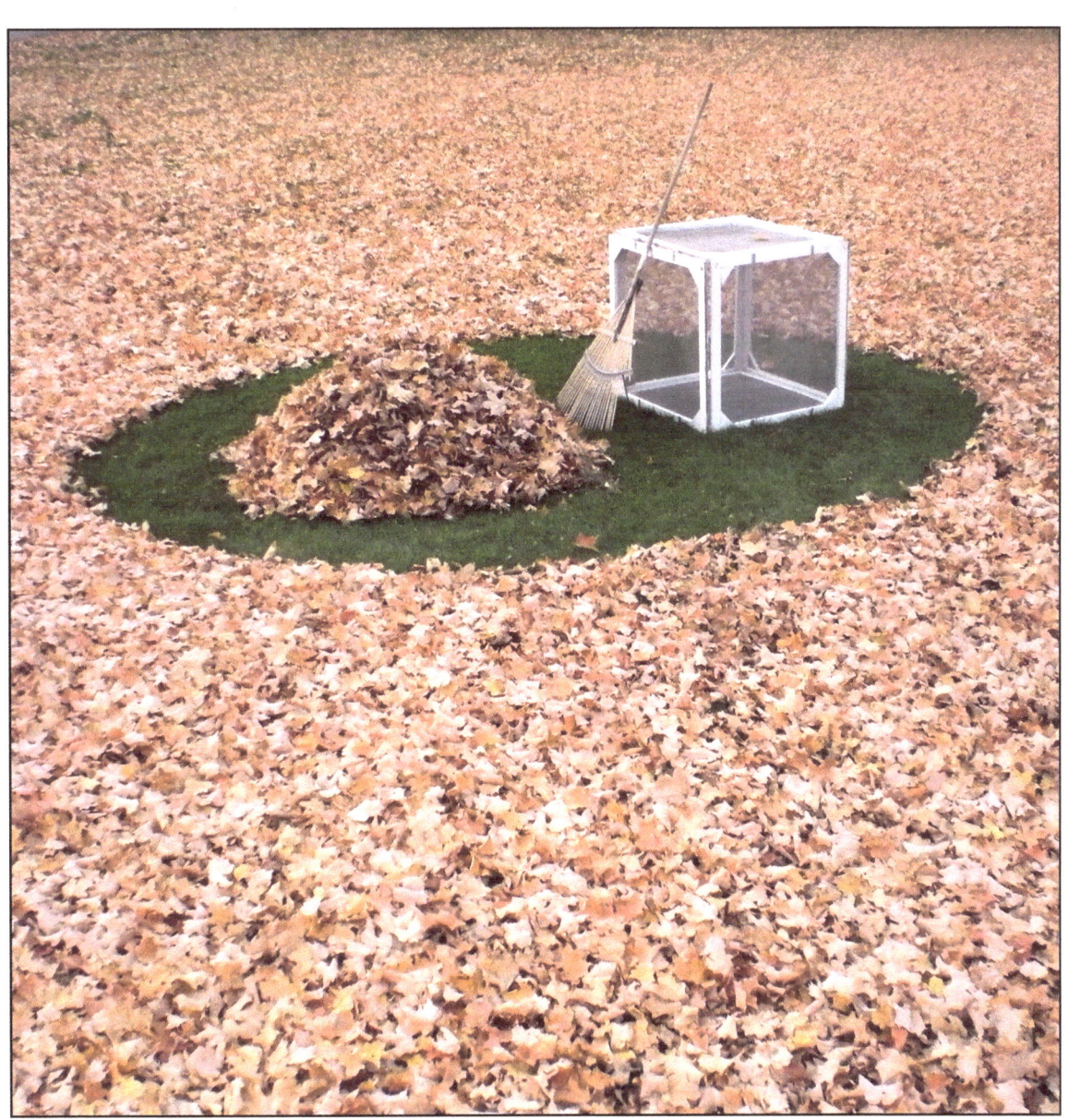

It's never not wood season.

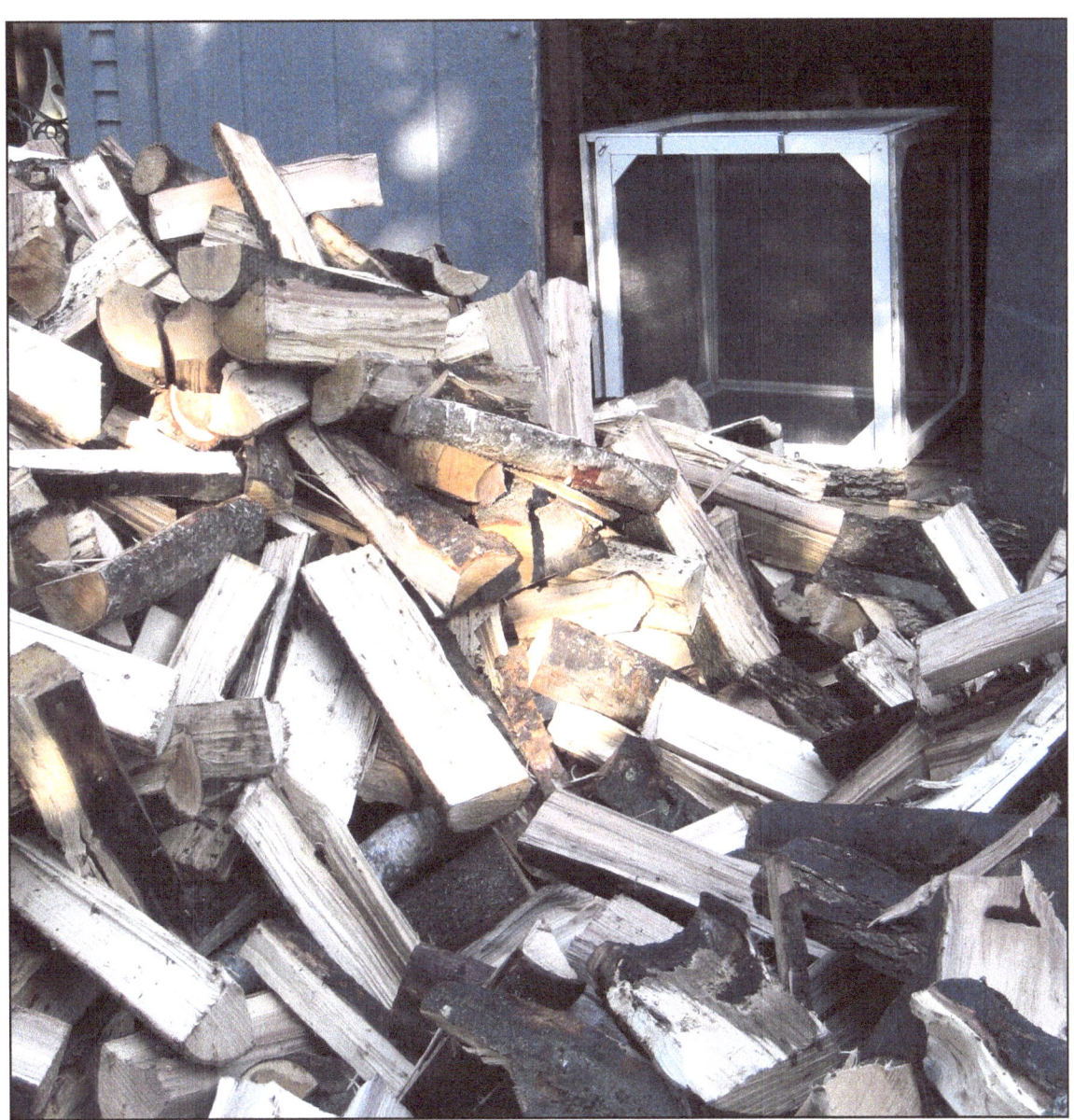

Tough D, Cube!

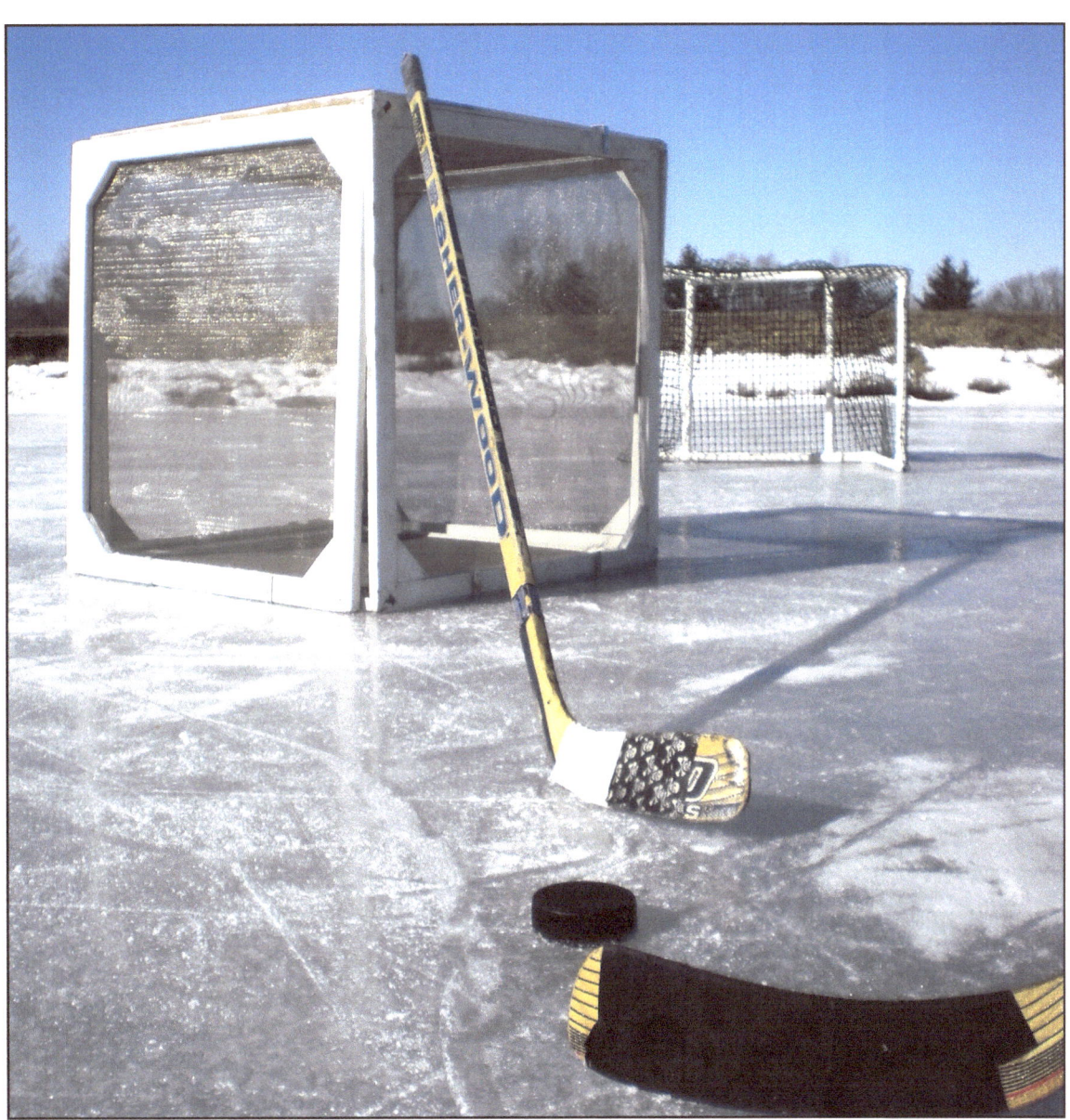

www.ingramcontent.com/pod-product-compliance
Lightning Source LLC
Chambersburg PA
CBHW051110180526
45172CB00002B/847